The Sirtfood Diet Cookbook

How to burn fat Naturally with an Exclusive and Unconventional Diet That Will Keep You Healthy by Activating Your "Skinny Gene". Burn fat and Lose Weight

Kate Matten

Table of Contents

Explanation of Sirt Food Diet

What is The Sirtfood Diet?

Launched originally in 2016, the Sirtfood diet remains a hot topic and involves followers adopting a diet rich in 'sirtfoods'. According to the diet's founders, these special foods work by activating specific proteins in the body called sirtuins. Sirtuins are believed to protect cells in the body from dying when they are under stress and are thought to regulate inflammation, metabolism, and the aging process. It's thought that sirtuins influence the body's ability to burn fat and boost metabolism, resulting in a seven-pound weight loss a week while maintaining muscle. However, some experts believe this is unlikely to be solely fat loss, but will instead reflect changes in glycogen stores from skeletal muscle and the liver.

So What Are These Magical 'Sirtfoods'? The Twenty Most Common Include:

- ❖ kale
- ❖ red wine
- ❖ strawberries
- ❖ onions
- ❖ soy

- ❖ parsley
- ❖ extra virgin olive oil
- ❖ dark chocolate (85% cocoa)
- ❖ matcha green tea
- ❖ buckwheat
- ❖ turmeric
- ❖ walnuts
- ❖ arugula (rocket)
- ❖ bird's eye chili
- ❖ lovage
- ❖ Medjool dates
- ❖ red chicory
- ❖ blueberries
- ❖ capers
- ❖ coffee

The diet is divided into two phases; the initial phase lasts one week and involves restricting calories to 1000kcal for three days, consuming three sirtfood green juices, and one meal rich in sirtfoods each day. The juices include kale, celery, rocket, parsley, green tea, and lemon. Meals include turkey escalope with sage, capers and parsley, chicken and kale curry, and prawn stir-fry with buckwheat noodles. From days four to seven, energy intakes are increased to 1500kcal comprising of two sirtfood green juices and two sirtfood-rich meals a day. Although the diet promotes healthy foods, it's restrictive in both your food choices and daily calories, especially during the initial stages. It also involves drinking juice, with the amounts suggested during phase one exceeding the current daily guidelines.

The second phase is known as the maintenance phase which lasts 14 days where steady weight loss occurs. The authors believe it's a sustainable and realistic way to lose weight. However, focusing on weight loss is not what the diet is all about – it's designed to be about eating the best foods nature has to offer. Long term they recommend eating three balanced sirtfood rich meals a day along with one sirtfood green juice.

Dietitian Emer Delaney Says:

'At first glance, this is not a diet I would advise for my clients. Aiming to have 1000kcal for three consecutive days is extremely difficult and I believe the majority of people would be unable to achieve it. Looking at the list of foods, you can see they are the sort of items that often appear on a 'healthy food list', however it would be better to encourage these as part of a healthy balanced diet. Having a glass of red wine or a small amount of chocolate occasionally won't do us any harm – I wouldn't recommend them daily. We should also be eating a mixture of different fruits and vegetables and not just those on the list.

'In terms of weight loss and boosting metabolism, people may have experienced a seven-pound weight loss on the scales, but in my experience, this will be fluid. Burning and losing fat takes time so it is extremely unlikely this weight loss is a loss of fat. I would be very cautious of any diet that recommends fast and sudden weight loss as this simply isn't achievable and will more than likely be a loss of fluid. As soon as people return to their regular eating habits, they will regain the weight. Slow and steady weight loss is the key and for this, we need to restrict calories and increase our activity levels. Eating balanced regular meals made up of low GI foods, lean protein, fruit, and vegetables, and keeping well hydrated is the safest way to lose weight.'

Breakfast Recipes

---

1. Any Berry Sauce

Prep Time: 5 minutes

Cooking Time: 15 minutes

Makes: 2¼ cups

Nutrition Facts

❖ For a Serving Size of 1 oz

❖ Calories 30 - Calories from Fat 0 (0%)

❖ Total Fat 0g

- ❖ Sodium 0%
- ❖ Carbohydrates 7g
- ❖ Net carbs 6g
- ❖ Fiber 1g 4%
- ❖ Protein 0g
- ❖ Vitamins and minerals 0mg
- ❖ Fatty acids 0mg
- ❖ Amino acids 0mg

The Percent Daily Values are based on a 2,000 calorie diet, so your values may change depending on your calorie needs

Ingredients

- ❖ 1/4 cup cold water
- ❖ 1 Tablespoon cornstarch
- ❖ 1/3 cup sugar
- ❖ 4 cups berries, fresh or frozen (blackberries, raspberries, blueberries, sliced strawberries, or a mixture)

Directions

- ❖ In a medium saucepan, mix sugar, cornstarch, water, and 2 cups of berries. Mash berries if desired.

- ❖ Heat over medium heat, stirring frequently, until the sauce starts to thicken.
- ❖ Remove from heat and stir in remaining berries.
- ❖ Mash if desired.
- ❖ Serve over pancakes, waffles, oatmeal, or yogurt.
- ❖ Refrigerate leftovers within 2 hours, for up to a week.

Notes:

1. Serve with Favorite Pancakes or Applesauce French Toast.

2. To freeze the sauce, replace the cornstarch in the recipe with Clearjel or Clear Jel, a special type of cornstarch.

---

2. Apple Bars

Prep Time: 15 minutes

Cooking Time: 45 minutes

Makes: 12 bars (3 x 4-inches

Nutritional Facts

- ❖ Calories: 230
- ❖ Total Fat: 8g
- ❖ Sodium: 180mg

- ❖ Carbohydrates: 38g
- ❖ Sugars: 26g
- ❖ Protein: 3g
- ❖ Dietary Fiber: 3g

Ingredients

- ❖ 1/2 cup all-purpose flour
- ❖ 1/2 cup whole-wheat flour
- ❖ 1/4 teaspoon salt
- ❖ 1/2 teaspoon baking soda
- ❖ 1/2 cup brown sugar
- ❖ 1 cup old fashioned rolled oats
- ❖ 1/2 teaspoon cinnamon
- ❖ 1/2 teaspoon nutmeg
- ❖ 1 pinch ground cloves (optional)
- ❖ 1/2 cup margarine or butter
- ❖ 3 cups apples, peeled, cored, and sliced (about 2 medium apples [3" diameter])
- ❖ 2/3 cup raisins
- ❖ 1/4 cup sugar

Directions

- ❖ Preheat oven to 350 degrees F. Lightly grease a 9x13-inch baking pan.

- ❖ Mix flour, salt, and baking soda together in a large bowl. Add brown sugar, oats, cinnamon, nutmeg, and ground cloves.
- ❖ Cut in butter or margarine with a pastry blender or 2 knives until mixture is crumbly.
- ❖ Spread half of the crumb mixture in the baking pan. Top with apple slices and raisins and sprinkle with sugar. Spread remaining crumb mixture evenly over apples.
- ❖ Bake at 350 degrees for 40 to 50 minutes. Cool and cut into 12 bars.

Notes

- ❖ Substitute ripe pears for apples
- ❖ Serve warm topped with vanilla yogurt

3. Apple Spice Baked Oatmeal

Prep Time: 10 minutes

Cooking Time: 30 minutes

Makes: 9 squares (2.5 inches x 2.5 inches)

Nutritional facts

Apple Spice Baked Oatmeal

- ❖ Calories: 195.9
- ❖ Protein: 5g
- ❖ Carbohydrates: 28.2g
- ❖ Exchange Other Carbs: 2
- ❖ Dietary Fiber: 4.6g
- ❖ Sugars: 12.8g

- ❖ Fat: 8g
- ❖ Saturated Fat: 1g
- ❖ Cholesterol: 31mg
- ❖ Vitamin A Iu: 123.3IU
- ❖ Niacin Equivalents: 1.6mg
- ❖ Vitamin B6: 0.1mg
- ❖ Vitamin C: 1mg
- ❖ Folate: 15.7mcg
- ❖ Calcium: 66.9mg
- ❖ Iron: 1.5mg
- ❖ Magnesium: 55.1mg
- ❖ Potassium: 236mg
- ❖ Sodium: 36.6mg
- ❖ Thiamin: 0.2mg
- ❖ Calories From Fat: 72
- ❖ Percent Of Calories From Carbs: 55
- ❖ Percent Of Calories From Fat: 35
- ❖ Percent Of Calories From Protein: 9
- ❖ Percent Of Calories From Sat Fat: 4

Percent Daily Values are based on a 2,000 calorie diet. Your daily values may be higher or lower depending on your calorie needs.

Ingredients

- ❖ 1 egg, beaten
- ❖ 1/2 cup applesauce
- ❖ 1 1/2 cups nonfat or 1% milk
- ❖ 1 teaspoon vanilla
- ❖ 2 Tablespoons oil
- ❖ 1 apple, chopped (about 1 ½ cups)
- ❖ 2 cups old fashioned rolled oats
- ❖ 1 teaspoon baking powder
- ❖ 1/4 teaspoon salt
- ❖ 1 teaspoon cinnamon

Topping

- ❖ 2 Tablespoons brown sugar
- ❖ 2 Tablespoons chopped nuts (optional)

Directions

- ❖ Preheat oven to 375 degrees. Lightly oil or spray an 8" x 8" baking dish.
- ❖ Combine the egg, applesauce, milk, vanilla, and oil in a bowl. Mix in the apple.
- ❖ In a separate bowl, mix the rolled oats, baking powder, salt, and cinnamon. Add to the liquid ingredients and mix well.

- ❖ Pour mixture into a baking dish, and bake for 25 minutes.
- ❖ Remove from oven and sprinkle with brown sugar and (optional) nuts.
- ❖ Return to oven and broil for 3 to 4 minutes until the top is browned and the sugar bubbles.
- ❖ Serve warm. Refrigerate leftovers within 2 hours.

Notes

- ❖ Substitute other fruit for the apple. Try bananas, pears, blueberries, or a mixture.
- ❖ Serve warm topped with vanilla yogurt.

4. Apple Spice Oatmeal

Prep Time: 5 minutes

Cooking Time: 10 minutes

Makes: 2 cups

Nutrition Facts

❖ Calories: 312
❖ Total Fat: 2.9 g
❖ Saturated Fat: 0.5 g
❖ Calories from Fat: 8.4%
❖ Cholesterol: 0 mg
❖ Protein: 7 g

- ❖ Carbohydrate: 66 g
- ❖ Sugar: 32.9 g
- ❖ Fiber: 4.7 g
- ❖ Sodium: 29 mg
- ❖ Calcium: 51 mg
- ❖ Iron: 2.8 mg
- ❖ Vitamin C: 2.1 mg
- ❖ Beta-Carotene: 0 mcg
- ❖ Vitamin E: 0.3 mg

Ingredients

- ❖ 1 apple
- ❖ 2 cups nonfat or 1% milk or water
- ❖ 1 cup quick-cooking or old fashioned rolled oats
- ❖ 1/8 teaspoon salt
- ❖ 1/8 teaspoon cinnamon
- ❖ 1 Tablespoon brown sugar
- ❖ 1/8 teaspoon nutmeg (optional)

Directions

- ❖ Rinse the apple, remove the core and cut into small chunks (about 1 ½ cups).
- ❖ Bring the water or milk to a boil in a saucepan.

❖ Add the oatmeal, salt, and apple chunks. Cook over medium heat for 1 minute if using quick-cooking oats or 7 to 10 minutes if using old fashioned rolled oats. Stir a couple of times while cooking.

❖ Remove from heat. Stir in cinnamon, brown sugar, and nutmeg, if desired.

❖ Refrigerate leftovers within 2 hours.

Notes

❖ To increase the apple flavor, use apple juice for all or part of the water. Mixing apple juice with milk may cause milk to curdle.

❖ Add bite-size dried fruit pieces like raisins, apricots, or cranberries in step 3, or sprinkle on top when serving.

❖ Sprinkle chopped nuts on top when serving.

5. Applesauce French Toast

Prep Time: 5 minutes

Cooking Time: 10 minutes

Makes: 6 slices

Nutritional Faacts

- ❖ Calories 30
- ❖ Fat   0.22 g
- ❖ Protein 2 g
- ❖ Carbohydrates 58 g
- ❖ Fiber 3 g

- ❖ Potassium   663 mg
- ❖ Vitamin C   23 mg
- ❖ Vitamin A   63 ug
- ❖ Vitamin B-6   0.29 mg
- ❖ Magnesium   57 mg

Ingredients

- ❖ 2 eggs
- ❖ 1/2 cup nonfat or 1% milk
- ❖ 1 teaspoon ground cinnamon
- ❖ 2 teaspoons white sugar
- ❖ 1/2 teaspoon vanilla
- ❖ 1/4 cup unsweetened applesauce
- ❖ 6 slices whole-wheat bread

Directions

- ❖ In a large mixing bowl, combine eggs, milk, cinnamon, sugar, vanilla, and applesauce. Mix well.
- ❖ Soak bread one slice at a time until the mixture is slightly absorbed.
- ❖ Lightly spray or oil a skillet or griddle. Cook over medium heat until golden brown on both sides.
- ❖ Serve hot.
- ❖ Refrigerate leftovers within 2 hours.

Notes

❖ To use sweetened applesauce, remove about 3/4 teaspoon of sugar from the measured amount.

❖ Top with applesauce, fresh fruit, or yogurt.

---

6. Baked Berry Oatmeal

Prep Time: 15 minutes

Cooking Time: 30 minutes

Makes: 6 cups

Nutrition Facts

❖ Calories: 389

❖ Water: 8%

❖ Protein: 16.9 grams

❖ Carbs: 66.3 grams

❖ Sugar: 0 grams

❖ Fiber: 10.6 grams

❖ Fat: 6.9 grams

Ingredients

❖ 2 cups old-fashioned rolled oats

❖ 1 teaspoon baking powder

❖ 1 teaspoon cinnamon

- ❖ 1/4 teaspoon salt
- ❖ 2 eggs
- ❖ 1/2 cup brown sugar
- ❖ 1 1/2 teaspoons vanilla
- ❖ 2 cups nonfat or 1% milk
- ❖ 4 teaspoons margarine or butter, melted
- ❖ 2 cups cane berries, fresh or frozen (raspberries, blackberries, marionberries)
- ❖ 1/4 cup walnuts, chopped (optional)

Directions

- ❖ preheat oven to 375 degrees F.
- ❖ In a medium bowl, mix the oats, baking powder, cinnamon, and salt.
- ❖ In a separate bowl beat the eggs until blended; Stir in brown sugar, vanilla, milk, and melted butter.
- ❖ Pour wet ingredients into the dry ingredients and stir until well combined.
- ❖ Add the berries and stir lightly to evenly distribute. Pour mixture into a 2-quart baking dish. Sprinkle with chopped nuts if desired.
- ❖ Bake for 20-30 minutes or until the top is golden brown.
- ❖ Refrigerate leftovers within 2 hours.

7. Banana Oatmeal Cookies

Prep Time: 10 minutes

Cooking Time: 15 minutes

Makes: 14 cookies

Nutrition Facts

- ❖ Calories 66.8
- ❖ Total Fat 2.5 g
- ❖ Saturated Fat 1.0 g
- ❖ Polyunsaturated Fat 0.7 g
- ❖ Monounsaturated Fat   0.6 g
- ❖ Cholesterol   4.0 mg

- ❖ Sodium 55.5 mg
- ❖ Potassium   61.5 mg
- ❖ Total Carbohydrate 12.2 g
- ❖ Dietary Fiber 0.5 g
- ❖ Sugars 7.4 g
- ❖ Protein 1.1 g

The Percent Daily Values are based on a 2,000 calorie diet, so your values may change depending on your calorie needs.

Ingredients

- ❖ 2 very ripe bananas
- ❖ 1 cup oats (quick or old-fashioned)
- ❖ 1/2 teaspoon cinnamon
- ❖ 1/2 teaspoon vanilla
- ❖ 1/2 cup raisins

Directions

- ❖ Preheat oven to 350 degrees.
- ❖ In a medium bowl, mash bananas with a fork until mostly smooth.
- ❖ Add oats, cinnamon, vanilla, and raisins. Mix well.

❖ Drop spoonfuls of dough onto a lightly sprayed or oiled baking sheet. Flatten with the back of a spoon or bottom of a drinking glass.

❖ Bake 10 to 15 minutes. Remove from oven and let cool before serving.

Notes

❖ The texture will be best when freshly made.

❖ Try dried cranberries or chopped nuts instead of raisins.

8. Very Berry Muesli ('mew-slee')

Prep Time: 5 minutes

Chill Time: 6 to 12 hours

Makes: 5 cups

Nutritional Facts

❖ Calories: 210
❖ Calories From Fat: 50

- ❖ Total Fat: 6g
- ❖ Sodium: 50mg
- ❖ Carbohydrates: 32g
- ❖ Sugars: 19g
- ❖ Protein: 7g
- ❖ Dietary Fiber: 3g

Ingredients

- ❖ 1 cup low-fat fruit yogurt
- ❖ 1 cup old fashioned rolled oats (raw)
- ❖ ½ cup nonfat or 1% milk
- ❖ ½ cup dried fruit (try raisins, apricots, dates)
- ❖ ½ cup chopped apple (about 1/3 a medium apple [3" diameter])
- ❖ ½ cup frozen blueberries
- ❖ ¼ cup chopped, toasted walnuts

Instructions

- ❖ In medium bowl, mix oats, yogurt, and milk.
- ❖ Cover and refrigerate for 6 to 12 hours.
- ❖ Add dried and fresh fruit, and mix gently.
- ❖ Serve scoops of muesli in small dishes. Sprinkle each serving with chopped nuts.
- ❖ Refrigerate leftovers within 2 hours.

Notes

❖ Muesli makes a delicious breakfast. Try drizzling with milk.

❖ Substitute any frozen, canned/drained, or fresh chopped fruit for apples and blueberries.

❖ Flavor boosters: cinnamon, grated orange peel.

Lunch Recipes

9. Asparagus Mushroom Melt

Prep Time: 15 minutes

Cooking Time: 15 minutes

Makes: 8 muffin halves

Nutritional Facts

❖ Calories: 152
❖ Sugar: 1.3 g
❖ Sodium: 742.8 mg
❖ Fat: 8.8 g

- ❖ Saturated Fat: 1.5 g
- ❖ Unsaturated Fat: 5.9 g
- ❖ Carbohydrates: 8.7 g
- ❖ Fiber: 3.1 g
- ❖ Protein: 10.7 g

Ingredients

- ❖ 4 English muffins
- ❖ 1/4 cup onion, finely minced
- ❖ 1 cup mushrooms, chopped
- ❖ 1 1/2 teaspoons oil
- ❖ 1/2 pound asparagus, trimmed and sliced crosswise into 1/2 inch rounds
- ❖ 1/2 teaspoon ground thyme or oregano or basil
- ❖ 1 1/2 teaspoons vinegar
- ❖ Dash of salt and pepper
- ❖ 3/4 cup mozzarella cheese, shredded (3 ounces)

Directions

- ❖ Toast muffin halves and place on a baking sheet in a single layer.
- ❖ In a large skillet over medium-high heat, sauté onions and mushrooms in oil, stirring often, until just beginning to brown.

- ❖ Add asparagus, seasoning, and vinegar. Sauté, stirring often, until asparagus is barely tender. Season lightly with salt and pepper.
- ❖ Divide the vegetable mixture equally onto the muffin halves. Top each muffin with shredded cheese.
- ❖ Broil muffins until the cheese melts. Watch carefully to avoid burning.
- ❖ Refrigerate leftovers within 2 hours.

10.　Autumn Squash Bisque With Ginger

Prep Time: 15 minutes

Cooking Time: 45 minutes

Makes: 10 cups

Nutritional Facts

- ❖ Calories: 80
- ❖ Calories From Fat: 10
- ❖ Total Fat: 1.5g
- ❖ Sodium: 340mg
- ❖ Carbohydrates: 18g
- ❖ Sugars: 6g
- ❖ Protein: 2g
- ❖ Dietary Fiber: 3g

Percent Daily Values are based on a 2,000 calorie diet. Your daily values may be higher or lower depending on your calorie needs.

Ingredients

- ❖ 2 teaspoons oil
- ❖ 2 cups sliced onions
- ❖ 2 pounds winter squash, peeled, seeded, and cut into 2-inch cubes (4 generous cups)
- ❖ 2 pears, peeled, cored, and diced, or 1 can (15 ounces) sliced pears, drained and chopped
- ❖ 2 cloves garlic, peeled and crushed
- ❖ 2 Tablespoons coarsely chopped, peeled fresh ginger, or 1 teaspoon powdered ginger
- ❖ 1/2 teaspoon thyme
- ❖ 4 cups chicken or vegetable broth (see notes)
- ❖ 1 cup of water
- ❖ 1 Tablespoon lemon juice
- ❖ 1/2 cup plain nonfat yogurt

Directions

- ❖ Heat oil in a large pot over medium heat.
- ❖ Add onions and cook, stirring constantly until softened, 3 to 4 minutes.

- ❖ Add squash, pears, garlic, ginger, and thyme; cook, stirring, for 1 minute.
- ❖ Add broth and water; bring to a simmer.
- ❖ Reduce heat to low, cover, and simmer until squash is tender 35-45 minutes.
- ❖ Puree soup, in batches, if necessary, in a blender. (If using a blender, follow manufacturer's directions for pureeing hot liquids.)
- ❖ Return soup to pot and heat through. Stir in lemon juice.
- ❖ Garnish each serving with a spoonful of yogurt.
- ❖ Refrigerate leftovers within 2 hours.

Notes

- ❖ Broth can be canned or made using bouillon. For each cup of broth use 1 cup very hot water and 1 teaspoon or 1 cube bouillon
- ❖ Freeze extra lemon juice to use later.

11. Baked Bean Medley

Prep Time: 15 minutes

Cooking Time: 1 1/2 hours

Makes: 8 cups

Nutritional Facts

❖ Calories 42

❖ Calories from Fat 11.7

❖ Total Fat 1.3g

❖ Saturated fat 0.5g

- ❖ Sodium 32mg
- ❖ Carbohydrates 6.9g
- ❖ Net carbs 6.5g
- ❖ Fiber 0.4g
- ❖ Glucose 3.3g
- ❖ Protein 0.5g

The Percent Daily Values are based on a 2,000 calorie diet, so your values may change depending on your calorie needs

Ingredients

- ❖ 6 slices bacon
- ❖ 1 cup chopped onion
- ❖ 1 clove garlic, minced or 1/4 teaspoon garlic powder
- ❖ 1 can (15 ounces) pinto beans, drained and rinsed
- ❖ 1 can (15 ounces) great northern beans, drained and rinsed
- ❖ 1 can (16 ounces) kidney beans, drained and rinsed
- ❖ 1 can (15 ounces) garbanzo beans, drained and rinsed
- ❖ 1 can (15 ounces) pork and beans
- ❖ 3/4 cup ketchup
- ❖ 1/4 cup molasses
- ❖ 1/4 cup brown sugar
- ❖ 2 Tablespoons Worcestershire sauce

- ❖ 1 Tablespoon prepared mustard
- ❖ 1/4 teaspoon pepper

Directions

- ❖ Preheat oven to 375 degrees.
- ❖ Cut bacon into bite-sized pieces and place in skillet. Cook over medium heat (300 degrees in an electric skillet) until evenly browned. Remove from pan and set aside.
- ❖ Drain skillet, reserving 1 teaspoon of drippings. Add onion and garlic. Cook until onion is tender. Remove from skillet and add to bacon. Discard remaining drippings.
- ❖ Mix beans with bacon, onion, and garlic. Stir in remaining ingredients.
- ❖ Transfer to a 9x12 baking dish or 3-quart casserole dish. Bake in a preheated oven for 1 hour.
- ❖ Refrigerate leftovers within 2 hours.

Notes

- ❖ Use any mix of beans you have.
- ❖ Cook your dry beans. One can (15 ounces) is about 1 1/2 to 1 3/4 cups drained beans.

❖ No bacon? Use 1 teaspoon cooking oil to saute vegetables.

---

12. Barley Summer Salad

Prep Time: 10 minutes

Cooking Time: 45 minutes

Makes: 8 cups

Nutrition Facts

❖ Calories 428

❖ Calories from Fat 99

❖ Fat 11g

❖ Saturated Fat 7g

❖ Cholesterol 44mg

❖ Sodium 581mg

❖ Potassium 575mg

❖ Carbohydrates 68g

❖ Fiber 13g

❖ Sugar 6g

❖ Protein 16g

❖ Vitamin A 535IU

❖ Vitamin C 28.7mg

❖ Calcium 290mg

- ❖ Iron 3.2mg

Percent Daily Values are based on a 2000 calorie diet.

Ingredients

- ❖ 1 cup dry barley
- ❖ 3 cups of water
- ❖ 1/4 cup dried cranberries
- ❖ 1 cup fresh blueberries
- ❖ 1 cup sweet snap peas, chopped
- ❖ 2 cups apples or another fresh fruit or veggie, chopped (about 1 1/3 medium apples [3" diameter])
- ❖ 1/2 cup red bell pepper, seeded and chopped (about 1 small pepper)
- ❖ 1/2 cup green onions, sliced thin
- ❖ 1 Tablespoon vinegar
- ❖ 3 Tablespoons oil
- ❖ 1/4 cup lemon or lime juice

Directions

- ❖ Place barley and water in a 2 or 3-quart saucepan. Bring to a boil, then turn to low. Cook covered for 45 minutes.
- ❖ Rinse cooked barley briefly in cold water. Drain.
- ❖ Add remaining ingredients. Toss well.

❖ Refrigerate leftovers within 2 hours.

Notes

❖ Substitute different fruits and vegetables in season.

❖ Add nuts or seeds for added protein.

---

13. Barley, Bean, And Corn Salad

Prep Time: 15 minutes

Cooking Time: 45 minutes

Makes: 6 cups

Nutrition Facts

- ❖ Calories 256
- ❖ Calories from Fat 72
- ❖ Fat 8g
- ❖ Saturated Fat 1g
- ❖ Cholesterol 0mg
- ❖ Sodium 245mg
- ❖ Potassium 0mg
- ❖ Carbohydrates 40g
- ❖ Fiber 9g
- ❖ Sugar 5g
- ❖ Protein 9g
- ❖ Net carbs 31g

Percent Daily Values are based on a 2000 calorie diet.

Ingredients

- ❖ 2 cups cooked barley (cooking directions below)
- ❖ 1 can (15 ounces) kidney beans, drained
- ❖ 1 cup corn (canned and drained, frozen, or fresh cooked)
- ❖ 1 large red bell pepper, seeded and finely chopped
- ❖ 1/2 cup sliced celery
- ❖ 1/4 cup sliced green onion

- ❖ 1 clove garlic, finely chopped or 1/4 teaspoon garlic powder
- ❖ 1/4 cup fresh lemon or lime juice
- ❖ 2 tablespoons oil
- ❖ Salt and pepper to taste
- ❖ Fresh cilantro or parsley sprigs, for garnish (optional)

Directions

- ❖ Mix barley with remaining ingredients, except garnish, in a large bowl.
- ❖ Cover and chill several hours or overnight to allow flavors to blend.
- ❖ Garnish with cilantro or parsley sprigs, if desired, and serve.
- ❖ Refrigerate leftovers within 2 hours.

Notes

- ❖ One large ear of corn makes about 1 cup of cut corn.
- ❖ Freeze extra lime or lemon juice to use later.
- ❖ Cook your dry beans. One can (15 ounces) is about 1 1/2 to 1 3/4 cups drained beans.

14. Beef Barley Soup

Prep Time: 15 minutes

Cooking Time: 45 minutes

Makes: 14 cups

Nutritional Facts

- ❖ Calories 90
- ❖ Calories from Fat 27
- ❖ Total Fat 3g
- ❖ Cholesterol 11mg
- ❖ Sodium 728mg
- ❖ Carbohydrates 11g
- ❖ Net carbs 9.4g
- ❖ Fiber 1.6g
- ❖ Glucose 0.6g
- ❖ Protein 5g
- ❖ Iron 0.2mg

The Percent Daily Values are based on a 2,000 calorie diet, so your values may change depending on your calorie needs.

Ingredients

- ❖ 1 pound lean ground beef (15% fat or less)
- ❖ 1 large carrot, diced, about 1 cup
- ❖ 1 small onion, diced, about 1 cup
- ❖ 2 stalk celery, diced, about 1 cup
- ❖ 2 cloves garlic, finely chopped or 1/2 teaspoon garlic powder
- ❖ 8 cups of water
- ❖ 2 teaspoons beef bouillon
- ❖ 1 can (14.5 ounces) diced tomatoes with juice
- ❖ 1 cup uncooked barley
- ❖ 1/2 teaspoon pepper

Directions

- ❖ In a large saucepot, cook ground beef over medium heat. Drain fat.
- ❖ Add carrots, onion, celery, and garlic; stir often and cook for about 5 minutes.
- ❖ Add 8 cups of water, bouillon, tomatoes with juice, barley, and pepper. Bring to a boil.
- ❖ Cover and reduce heat to a low boil. Cook for about 30 minutes or until barley is as tender as you like it.
- ❖ Serve immediately.
- ❖ Refrigerate leftovers within 2 hours.

Notes

❖ Add 1 cup sliced mushrooms with tomatoes.

❖ Add 1 cup chopped kale or other greens with tomatoes.

---

15. Bell Pepper Nachos

Prep Time: 5 minutes

Cooking Time: 15 minutes

Makes: 8 cups

Nutrition Facts

❖ Calories 764

❖ Calories from Fat 405

❖ Fat 45g

- ❖ Saturated Fat 15g
- ❖ Cholesterol 79mg
- ❖ Sodium 839mg
- ❖ Potassium 414mg
- ❖ Carbohydrates 64g
- ❖ Fiber 6g
- ❖ Sugar 2g
- ❖ Protein 27g
- ❖ Vitamin A 640IU
- ❖ Vitamin C 3.2mg
- ❖ Calcium 504mg
- ❖ Iron 3.6mg

Percent Daily Values are based on a 2000 calorie diet.

Ingredients

- ❖ 4 bell peppers
- ❖ 1 cup of salsa
- ❖ 2 teaspoons seasoning (try a mixture-chili powder, garlic powder, ground cumin, pepper)
- ❖ 2 cups cooked meat (chopped or shredded), beans or tofu
- ❖ 1/2 cup shredded cheese

Directions

- ❖ Preheat oven to 350 degrees F.
- ❖ Wash bell peppers, remove seeds, and cut into bite-size pieces. Arrange pieces close together in a single layer on a large foil-lined baking sheet.
- ❖ In a medium bowl, combine salsa, seasonings and meat, beans, or tofu. Spoon the mixture evenly over pepper pieces then top with cheese.
- ❖ Bake for 15 minutes, or until peppers are heated through and cheese is melted. Serve warm.
- ❖ Refrigerate leftovers within 2 hours.

Notes

- ❖ For added flavor, top with chopped cilantro, green onions, or black olives!

16. Black Bean Soup

Prep Time: 15 minutes

Cooking Time: 45 minutes

Makes: 12 cups

Nutritional Facts

- ❖ Calories: 349.4
- ❖ Protein: 16.2g
- ❖ Carbohydrates: 6.7g
- ❖ Exchange Other Carbs: 0.5
- ❖ Dietary Fiber: 1g
- ❖ Sugars: 2.3g
- ❖ Fat: 28.8g

- ❖ Saturated Fat: 13.6g
- ❖ Cholesterol: 67.8mg
- ❖ Vitamin A Iu: 2558.7IU
- ❖ Niacin Equivalents: 5.4mg
- ❖ Vitamin B6: 0.3mg
- ❖ Vitamin C: 34.6mg
- ❖ Folate: 16.6mcg
- ❖ Calcium: 227.6mg
- ❖ Iron: 0.8mg
- ❖ Magnesium: 23.5mg
- ❖ Potassium: 325.8mg
- ❖ Sodium: 1257.5mg
- ❖ Thiamin: 0.3mg
- ❖ Calories From Fat: 259.2

Percent Daily Values are based on a 2,000 calorie diet. Your daily values may be higher or lower depending on your calorie needs.

Ingredients

- ❖ 1 Tablespoon vegetable oil
- ❖ 1 small onion chopped (about 1 cup)
- ❖ 4 cloves garlic, minced or 1 teaspoon garlic powder
- ❖ 1 can (15 ounces) diced tomatoes

- ❖ 4 cups black beans, about 2 cans (15 ounces) cooked or canned (with liquid)
- ❖ 2 potatoes, peeled and diced
- ❖ 4 cups of water
- ❖ 1/2 cup fresh cilantro, chopped
- ❖ 1 Tablespoon cumin
- ❖ 1/3 cup lime juice or juice from 1 lime
- ❖ Hot sauce to taste

Directions

- ❖ Heat oil in a large pot over medium-high heat. Sauté the onion for 2 minutes. Add the garlic and tomatoes and cook for 2 minutes. Stir often.
- ❖ Add the beans, potatoes, and water. Bring to a boil; then reduce to medium-low heat. Cover and cook for 20 minutes.
- ❖ Add the cilantro, cumin, lime juice, and hot pepper sauce, if desired. Stir and cook for 10 minutes. Serve hot.
- ❖ Refrigerate leftovers within 2 hours.

Notes

- ❖ Try topping the soup with non-fat sour cream, chopped cilantro, and baked tortilla chips.
- ❖ Freeze extra lime juice to use later.

Dinner Recipes

17. Beef and Broccoli

Prep Time: 15 minutes

Cooking Time: 30 minutes

Makes: 7 cups

Nutritional Facts

- ❖ Calories 364
- ❖ Calories from Fat 234
- ❖ Fat 26g
- ❖ Saturated Fat 16g
- ❖ Cholesterol 74mg
- ❖ Sodium 559mg
- ❖ Potassium 529mg
- ❖ Carbohydrates 7g
- ❖ Fiber 1g
- ❖ Sugar 1g
- ❖ Protein 23g
- ❖ Vitamin A 355IU
- ❖ Vitamin C 51.1mg
- ❖ Calcium 36mg
- ❖ Iron 3.1mg17

Percent Daily Values are based on a 2000 calorie diet.

Ingredients

- ❖ 3/4 pound lean ground beef
- ❖ 1/4 teaspoon ground ginger
- ❖ 3/4 teaspoon garlic powder
- ❖ 2 Tablespoons brown sugar
- ❖ 1/4 cup low-sodium soy sauce
- ❖ 2 teaspoons cornstarch

- ❖ 1 Tablespoon sesame oil
- ❖ 1/4 teaspoon red pepper flakes
- ❖ 1/2 cup water
- ❖ 4 cups broccoli, chopped (fresh or frozen)
- ❖ 3 cups cooked bulgur

Directions

- ❖ Sauté beef, ginger, and garlic powder in a skillet over medium-high heat until meat is browned.
- ❖ In a bowl, mix sugar, soy sauce, cornstarch, sesame oil, pepper flakes, and water.
- ❖ Add sauce to beef and cook for 5 minutes. Add broccoli and cook until tender.
- ❖ Serve over cooked bulgur.
- ❖ Refrigerate leftovers within 2 hours.

18. Tasty Hamburger Skillet

Prep Time: 10 minutes

Cooking Time: 30 minutes

Makes: 9 cups

Nutritional Facts

- ❖ Calories: 270

- Calories From Fat: 70
- Total Fat: 8g
- Sodium: 240mg
- Carbohydrates: 33g
- Sugars: 3g
- Protein: 16g
- Dietary Fiber: 6g

Percent Daily Values are based on a 2,000 calorie diet. Your daily values may be higher or lower depending on your calorie needs.

Ingredients

- 1 pound lean ground beef (15% fat)
- ⅓ cup chopped onion (1/3 medium onion)
- ⅓ cup green pepper, chopped
- 2 cups water
- 1 cup long grain white rice
- 1 teaspoon garlic powder or 4 cloves of garlic
- 1 tablespoon chili powder
- ¼ teaspoon salt
- ¼ teaspoon ground pepper
- 1 can (15 ounces) diced tomatoes, with juice
- 1 ½ cups corn (canned and drained, frozen, or fresh cooked)

- ❖ 1 can (15 ounces) red kidney beans, drained and rinsed
- ❖ ½ cup grated cheddar cheese

Instructions

- ❖ Cook ground beef, onion, and green pepper in large skillet over medium heat (300 degrees in an electric skillet) until hamburger is no longer pink. Drain excess fat from pan.
- ❖ Add water, rice, garlic powder, chili powder, salt, pepper, tomatoes with juice, corn, and beans.
- ❖ Cook, covered, for about 20 minutes or until rice is soft.
- ❖ Remove from stove top, sprinkle with grated cheese, and serve hot.
- ❖ Refrigerate leftovers within 2 hours.

Notes

- ❖ Garnish this dish with a tablespoon of low-fat sour cream.
- ❖ Flavor boosters: green chilis, jalepeños, more garlic, and other seasonings.

- ❖ Make extra! Leftovers make a great filling for tacos, burritos, filling for stuffed bell peppers, or as a topping for baked potatoes.
- ❖ Use whole grains! Use brown rice instead of white rice and increase cooking time to 45 minutes or until rice is cooked.
- ❖ Cook your own dry beans. One can (15 ounces) is about 1 1/2 to 1 3/4 cups drained beans.

19. White Chicken Chili

Prep Time: 20 minutes

Cooking Time: 30 minutes

Makes: 8 cups

Nutritional Facts

- ❖ Calories: 300
- ❖ Calories From Fat: 70
- ❖ Total Fat: 10g
- ❖ Sodium: 580mg
- ❖ Carbohydrates: 30g
- ❖ Sugars: 5g
- ❖ Protein: 23g
- ❖ Dietary Fiber: 6g

Percent Daily Values are based on a 2,000 calorie diet. Your daily values may be higher or lower depending on your calorie needs.

Ingredients

- ❖ 1 tablespoon oil
- ❖ 1 pound boneless, skinless chicken breasts, cut bite-sized
- ❖ 1 onion, chopped
- ❖ 1 ½ teaspoons garlic powder or 6 cloves garlic
- ❖ 2 cans (15.5 ounces each) white beans, rinsed and drained
- ❖ 2 cups (or 14.5 ounce can) chicken broth (see notes)

- ❖ 2 cans (4 ounces each) chopped mild green chilies
- ❖ 1 teaspoon ground cumin
- ❖ 1 teaspoon dried oregano leaves
- ❖ ½ teaspoon pepper
- ❖ ¼ teaspoon cayenne pepper or chili powder (optional)
- ❖ 1 cup sour cream or plain yogurt
- ❖ ½ cup nonfat or 1% milk

Instructions

- ❖ Heat oil in a large saucepan; sauté the chicken, onion and garlic until chicken is no longer pink.
- ❖ Add the beans, broth, chilies and seasonings.
- ❖ Bring to a boil. Reduce heat; simmer uncovered, for 30 minutes.
- ❖ Remove from the heat; stir in sour cream and milk.
- ❖ Refrigerate leftovers within 2 hours.

Notes

- ❖ Broth can be canned or made using bouillon. For each cup of broth use 1 cup very hot water and 1 teaspoon or 1 cube bouillon.
- ❖ Instead of chicken use turkey or an additional 2 cups of cooked beans.

- ❖ Cook your own dry beans. One can (15 ounces) is about 1 1/2 to 1 3/4 cups drained beans.
- ❖ Serve with hot sauce or black pepper.

20. Black Bean Soup

Prep Time: 15 minutes

Cooking Time: 45 minutes

Makes: 12 cups

Nutritional Facts

- ❖ Calories 342
- ❖ Total Fat 6.1g
- ❖ Saturated Fat 1g
- ❖ Monounsaturated Fat 3.7g
- ❖ Sodium 1563.1mg
- ❖ Total Carbohydrate 56g
- ❖ Dietary Fiber 21.3g
- ❖ Sugars 4.2g
- ❖ Protein 18.7g

Ingredients

- ❖ 1 Tablespoon vegetable oil
- ❖ 1 small onion chopped (about 1 cup)
- ❖ 4 cloves garlic, minced or 1 teaspoon garlic powder
- ❖ 1 can (15 ounces) diced tomatoes
- ❖ 4 cups black beans, about 2 cans (15 ounces) cooked or canned (with liquid)
- ❖ 2 potatoes, peeled and diced
- ❖ 4 cups of water
- ❖ 1/2 cup fresh cilantro, chopped
- ❖ 1 Tablespoon cumin

- 1/3 cup lime juice or juice from 1 lime
- Hot sauce to taste

Directions

- Heat oil in a large pot over medium-high heat. Sauté the onion for 2 minutes. Add the garlic and tomatoes and cook for 2 minutes. Stir often.
- Add the beans, potatoes, and water. Bring to a boil; then reduce to medium-low heat. Cover and cook for 20 minutes.
- Add the cilantro, cumin, lime juice, and hot pepper sauce, if desired. Stir and cook for 10 minutes. Serve hot.
- Refrigerate leftovers within 2 hours.

Notes

- Try topping the soup with non-fat sour cream, chopped cilantro, and baked tortilla chips.
- Freeze extra lime juice to use later.

21. Cheesy Beef Pasta

Prep Time: 20 minutes

Cooking Time: 30 minutes

Makes: 8 cups

Nutritional Facts

- ❖ Calories: 398.3
- ❖ Protein: 13.9g
- ❖ Carbohydrates: 45.1g
- ❖ Dietary Fiber: 2.6g
- ❖ Sugars: 2.3g
- ❖ Fat: 17.5g
- ❖ Saturated Fat: 8.5g
- ❖ Folate: 106.9mcg
- ❖ Calcium: 172.9mg
- ❖ Iron: 2mg
- ❖ Magnesium: 33.2mg
- ❖ Potassium: 115mg
- ❖ Sodium: 276mg

Percent Daily Values are based on a 2,000 calorie diet. Your daily values may be higher or lower depending on your calorie needs.

Ingredients

- ❖ 1/2 pound lean ground beef (15% fat)
- ❖ 1 onion, diced (about 1 cup)
- ❖ 2 cloves garlic, minced, or 1/2 teaspoon garlic powder
- ❖ 1 small zucchini, chopped (about 1 1/2 cups)
- ❖ 1 jar (24 to 26 ounces) tomato-based pasta sauce
- ❖ 1/2 teaspoon dried basil
- ❖ 1/2 teaspoon dried oregano
- ❖ 1/4 teaspoon hot red pepper flakes (optional)
- ❖ 12 ounces rotini pasta (about 4 cups)
- ❖ 2 ounces shredded cheddar cheese (about 1/2 cup)
- ❖ 6 ounces shredded mozzarella cheese (about 1 1/2 cups)

Directions

- ❖ In a large skillet, cook beef, onion, garlic, and zucchini over medium-high heat (350 degrees in an electric skillet) until meat is browned and broken into pieces. Drain any fat.
- ❖ Add the pasta sauce, basil, oregano, and red pepper flakes, if desired. Bring to a simmer and cook on medium-low (275 degrees in an electric skillet) for 15 minutes.

- ❖ Cook the pasta in boiling water according to package directions.
- ❖ Drain the pasta and add to the sauce in the skillet. Stir in the cheese and cover until the cheese is melted.
- ❖ Refrigerate leftovers within 2 hours.

Notes

- ❖ Substitute broccoli for zucchini. Cook fresh broccoli with the pasta in step 3 or add frozen broccoli in step 2.

---

22.   Cheesy Polenta Pie

Prep Time: 30 minutes

Cooking Time: 30 minutes

Makes: 12 cups

Nutritional Facts

- ❖ Calories: 233.2
- ❖ Protein: 11.5g
- ❖ Carbohydrates: 22.3g
- ❖ Dietary Fiber: 2.9g
- ❖ Sugars: 7.4g
- ❖ Fat: 10.8g

- ❖ Saturated Fat: 5.7g
- ❖ Cholesterol: 25.2mg
- ❖ Vitamin A Iu: 649.5IU
- ❖ Niacin Equivalents: 4.6mg
- ❖ Vitamin B6: 0.2mg
- ❖ Vitamin C: 18.2mg
- ❖ Folate: 16.4mcg
- ❖ Calcium: 262.1mg
- ❖ Iron: 0.8mg
- ❖ Magnesium: 25.1mg
- ❖ Potassium: 291.5mg
- ❖ Sodium: 808.7mg

Percent Daily Values are based on a 2,000 calorie diet. Your daily values may be higher or lower depending on your calorie needs.

Ingredients

1. Filling

- ❖ 1/2 pound lean ground beef (15% fat)
- ❖ 1/2 medium onion, chopped (about 1/2 cup)
- ❖ 1 can (15.5 ounces) kidney beans, drained and rinsed
- ❖ 1 can (14.5 ounces) diced tomatoes with juice

* 1 1/2 cups corn (canned and drained, frozen, or fresh cooked)
* 1 Tablespoon chili powder
* 1/2 teaspoon cumin powder
* 1 teaspoon garlic powder or 4 cloves of garlic
* 1/2 teaspoon oregano
* 1/2 teaspoon salt
* 1/2 teaspoon pepper

2. Topping

* 1 cup yellow cornmeal
* 1 teaspoon salt
* 1 teaspoon sugar
* 1 teaspoon chili powder
* 2 1/2 cups water
* 1 cup grated cheddar cheese

Directions

* Brown meat and onion in a large skillet over medium-high heat (350 degrees in an electric skillet). Drain fat.
* Add beans, tomatoes, corn, 1 tablespoon chili powder, cumin, garlic powder, oregano, salt, and pepper.

- ❖ Reduce heat to low (250 degrees in an electric skillet), cover, and heat thoroughly.
- ❖ As chili heats, mix cornmeal, salt, sugar, and 1 teaspoon chili powder with water in a small saucepan.
- ❖ Cook over medium heat, stirring constantly until thickened, about 2 minutes. Add cheddar and mix well.
- ❖ Spread cornmeal mixture over chili mixture.
- ❖ Cover and cook over low heat, with lid slightly ajar, until topping is set, about 10 minutes.
- ❖ Refrigerate leftovers within 2 hours.

Notes

- ❖ Substitute 1-2 tablespoons taco seasoning mix for the last 6 ingredients in the filling.
- ❖ Cook your dry beans. One can (15 ounces) is about 1 1/2 to 1 3/4 cups drained beans.
- ❖ One large ear of corn makes about 1 cup of cut corn.

23.   Chicken And Black Bean Salsa Burritos

Prep Time: 20 minutes

Cooking Time: 30 minutes

Nutritional Facts

- ❖ Calories 355
- ❖ Fat 2g
- ❖ Sat fat 1g
- ❖ Protein 36g
- ❖ Carbohydrate 46g
- ❖ Fiber 9g
- ❖ Cholesterol 66mg
- ❖ Sodium 558mg
- ❖ Calcium 58mg

❖ Iron 3.8mg

Ingredients

❖ 1 can (15 ounces) black beans, drained and rinsed
❖ 2 green onions, chopped
❖ 1 Tablespoon lemon juice
❖ 1/4 teaspoon ground cumin
❖ 1/2 teaspoon salt, divided in half
❖ 4 boneless, skinless chicken breasts
❖ 1/4 teaspoon chili powder
❖ 1/4 teaspoon ground black pepper
❖ 1/2 cup shredded cheese, grated (try cheddar, pepper jack, or Mexican blend)
❖ 4 (9 inches) flour tortillas

Directions

❖ Preheat oven to 350 degrees.
❖ Combine the beans, green onions, lemon juice, cumin, and 1/4 teaspoon of the salt in a small bowl.
❖ Rub the chicken breasts with the chili powder, pepper, and the remaining 1/4 teaspoon salt.

* Cook the chicken in a skillet over medium-high heat (350 degrees in an electric skillet) for 5 minutes. Turn and cook until done, 4-5 minutes longer.
* Let chicken cool; slice into strips or chunks.
* Divide cheese evenly between tortillas. Top the cheese with equal amounts of chicken and black bean salsa mixture.
* Roll up the burritos and wrap each one in foil.
* Bake burritos until the cheese melts, about 15 minutes.
* Refrigerate leftovers within 2 hours.

Notes

* Freeze extra lemon juice to use later.
* Cook your dry beans. One can (15 ounces) is about 1 1/2 to 1 3/4 cups drained beans.

24. Chicken and Dumpling Casserole

Prep Time: 10 minutes

Cooking Time: 30 minutes

Makes: 8 cups

Nutritional Facts

- ❖ Calories: 441.2
- ❖ Protein: 16.8g
- ❖ Carbohydrates: 36.7g
- ❖ Exchange Other Carbs: 2.5
- ❖ Dietary Fiber: 0.9g
- ❖ Sugars: 1.7g
- ❖ Fat: 25g
- ❖ Saturated Fat: 12.2g
- ❖ Folate: 91.9mcg
- ❖ Calcium: 48.5mg
- ❖ Iron: 3.7mg
- ❖ Magnesium: 21.7mg
- ❖ Potassium: 194mg
- ❖ Sodium: 1211.2mg

Percent Daily Values are based on a 2,000 calorie diet. Your daily values may be higher or lower depending on your calorie needs.

Ingredients

- ❖ 3 Tablespoons oil
- ❖ 1 cup chopped onion (about 1 medium)
- ❖ 1 cup chopped carrots (about 2 small)
- ❖ 1 cup chopped celery (about 2 stalks)
- ❖ 3 cups low sodium chicken broth (see notes)
- ❖ 3 Tablespoons flour
- ❖ 2 cups cooked chicken, bite-sized
- ❖ 1 cup frozen peas
- ❖ salt and pepper (try 1/4 to 1/2 teaspoon)

Dumplings

- ❖ 1 cup flour
- ❖ 2 teaspoons baking powder
- ❖ 1/4 teaspoon salt
- ❖ 1 egg
- ❖ 1/3 cup nonfat or 1% milk

Directions

❖ Heat oil in a large skillet over medium-high heat (350 degrees in an electric skillet) and saute onions, carrots, and celery until soft.

❖ Add a small amount of unheated broth to the flour and stir until smooth. Slowly mix in remaining broth and add to skillet. Stir over medium heat as the mixture thickens.

❖ Add the chicken, peas, salt, and pepper. Heat on low while making dumplings.

❖ Dumplings: sift the flour, baking powder, and salt together into a mixing bowl.

❖ Add the egg to the milk and beat until well blended. Stir into the flour until well combined.

❖ Pour the chicken mixture into a lightly oiled or sprayed casserole dish. Drop dumpling dough by spoonfuls onto chicken mixture. (makes about 8 dumplings)

❖ Bake uncovered at 400 degrees for 15 minutes or until the dumplings are golden brown.

❖ Refrigerate leftovers within 2 hours.

Notes

❖ Broth can be canned or made using bouillon. For each cup of broth use 1 cup very hot water and 1 teaspoon or 1 cube bouillon.

Snack Recipes

25. Roasted Parsnips and Carrots

Prep Time: 5 minutes

Cooking Time: 30 minutes

Makes: 3 Cups

Nutritional Facts

- ❖ Calories: 90
- ❖ Calories From Fat 25
- ❖ Total Fat: 0g
- ❖ Sodium: 95mg

- ❖ Carbohydrates: 16g
- ❖ Sugars: 5g
- ❖ Protein: 1g
- ❖ Dietary Fiber: 4g

Ingredients

- ❖ ¾ pound parsnips, peeled
- ❖ ¾ pound carrots, peeled
- ❖ 1 tablespoon olive oil or vegetable oil
- ❖ ⅛ teaspoon salt
- ❖ ⅛ teaspoon garlic powder
- ❖ ⅛ teaspoon black pepper

Instructions

- ❖ Preheat oven to 400 degrees F.
- ❖ Cut the peeled parsnips and carrots into uniform pieces such as 3 inch x ½ inch sticks or 1 inch thick slices.
- ❖ Place cut parsnips and carrots into a large bowl. Add the vegetable oil and stir to coat the carrots and parsnips.
- ❖ In a small bowl stir together the salt, garlic powder and black pepper. Add to the carrots and parsnips

and stir until the vegetables are well coated with seasonings.

❖ Place vegetables in a single layer on large baking sheet being careful not to overcrowd the pan. Lining the baking sheet with foil or baking parchment will help with clean-up.

❖ Roast in the preheated oven for 20-30 minutes, stirring the vegetables half way through the time. The carrots and parsnips should be caramelized to a medium brown and blistered.

❖ Refrigerate leftovers within 2 hours.

26.   Whole Wheat Yogurt Rolls

Prep Time: 10 minutes

Cook Time: 15 minutes

Makes: 10 rolls

Nutritional Facts

❖ Calories: 80

❖ Total Fat: 1g

❖ Sodium: 470mg

❖ Carbohydrates: 15g

❖ Sugars: 2g

❖ Protein: 4g

❖ Dietary Fiber: 2g

Ingredients

❖ 1 ½ cups whole wheat flour

❖ 1 ¾ teaspoons baking soda

❖ 1 teaspoon salt

❖ 1 ¼ cups low-fat plain yogurt

Instructions

❖ Preheat oven to 450 degrees F.

❖ Stir flour, baking soda, and salt together in a large bowl. Add yogurt to the center and stir until a dough forms.

❖ Divide dough into 10 equal sized balls. Dust hands with flour and roll each ball lightly until surface is smoothed.

❖ Place on baking sheet and flatten each ball to ½ inch thick.

❖ Bake for 10 to 15 minutes, until light golden brown. Serve warm with a soup or salad.

27.   Tofu Banana Pudding

Prep Time: 15 minutes

Makes: 3 ½ Cups

Nutritional Facts

- ❖ Calories: 90
- ❖ Calories From Fat 15
- ❖ Total Fat: 1.5g
- ❖ Sodium: 0mg
- ❖ Carbohydrates: 16g
- ❖ Sugars: 10g
- ❖ Protein: 3g
- ❖ Dietary Fiber: 1g

Ingredients

- ❖ 16 ounces silken tofu
- ❖ 3 ripe bananas (mash 2, slice 1)
- ❖ 2 tablespoons sugar
- ❖ 1 teaspoon vanilla

Instructions

- ❖ Combine tofu, 2 mashed bananas, sugar, and vanilla. Blend until smooth.

- ❖ Pour into a serving bowl or dishes.
- ❖ Cover and refrigerate until chilled. Top with sliced banana just before serving.
- ❖ Refrigerate leftovers within 2 hours.

---

28.   Baked Apple Chips

Prep Time: 10 minutes

Cooking Time: 2 hours

Makes: 2 cups

Nutritional Facts

- ❖ Calories: 90

- ❖ Calories From Fat 5
- ❖ Total Fat: 0g
- ❖ Sodium: 0mg
- ❖ Carbohydrates: 25g
- ❖ Sugars: 19g
    - ❖ Protein: 0g
    - ❖ Dietary Fiber: 4g

Ingredients

- ❖ 2 large apples
- ❖ cinnamon (optional)

Directions

- ❖ Rinse apples and cut crosswise into thin slices. Cut out the core if desired.
- ❖ Arrange slices in a single layer on baking sheets. Sprinkle lightly with cinnamon if desired.
- ❖ Bake at 200 degrees F for about 1 hour. Turn slices over. Continue baking until dry with no moisture in the center, 1 hour or more depending on thickness.
- ❖ Remove from oven and cool. Store in an air-tight container for up to a year.

29. Baked Cauliflower Tots

Prep Time: 10 minutes

Cooking Time: 20 minutes

Makes: 2 cups

Nutritional Facts

- ❖ Calories: 70
- ❖ Calories From Fat 5
- ❖ Total Fat: 2.5g
- ❖ Sodium: 200mg
- ❖ Carbohydrates: 9g
- ❖ Sugars: 2g
- ❖ Protein: 5g
- ❖ Dietary Fiber: 2g

Ingredients

- ❖ 2 cups grated cauliflower (about half a medium head)
- ❖ 1 egg
- ❖ 3 Tablespoons flour
- ❖ 1/4 cup cheddar cheese, grated
- ❖ 1/4 teaspoon salt

Directions

❖ Preheat oven to 400 degrees. Spray a baking sheet or line with parchment paper or foil.

❖ Grate cauliflower on large holes of a grater.

❖ In a medium bowl, combine cauliflower, egg, flour, cheese, and salt; mix well.

❖ Press mixture together to make about 15 small balls or logs; Place on the baking sheet with space between each ball or log.

❖ Bake for 20 minutes or until cooked through. For extra crispy tots, broil for an extra 2 minutes. Watch closely to avoid burning.

❖ Refrigerate leftovers within 2 hours.

Notes

❖ The texture will be best when freshly made.

30.   Baked Cinnamon Tortilla Chips

Prep Time: 10 minutes

Cooking Time: 10 minutes

Makes: 24 chips

Nutritional Facts

- ❖ Calories: 150
- ❖ Calories From Fat 40
- ❖ Total Fat: 0g
- ❖ Sodium: 340mg
- ❖ Carbohydrates: 23g
- ❖ Sugars: 2g

- ❖ Protein: 4g
- ❖ Dietary Fiber: 3g

Ingredients

- ❖ 4 (8-inch) whole-wheat tortillas
- ❖ 2 teaspoons margarine or butter, melted or cooking spray
- ❖ 2 teaspoons cinnamon
- ❖ 2 teaspoons sugar

Directions

- ❖ Preheat the oven to 350 degrees F.
- ❖ Brush top of tortillas with melted butter/margarine or spray with cooking spray.
- ❖ Combine cinnamon and sugar in a small bowl. Sprinkle each tortilla lightly with the cinnamon mixture.
- ❖ Cut each tortilla into wedges or strips. Arrange the pieces in a single layer on a baking sheet.
- ❖ Bake until the edges are dry and crispy, 8 to 12 minutes. Watch closely to avoid burning. Chips will crisp more as they cool.
- ❖ Allow to cool and remove from pan.
- ❖ Store leftovers in a closed bag or container.

31. Baked Tomatoes With Cheese

Prep Time: 5 minutes

Cooking Time: 10 minutes

Makes: 8 1-inch slices

Nutritional Facts

* ❖ Calories: 50
* ❖ Calories From Fat 20
* ❖ Total Fat: 2g
* ❖ Sodium: 260mg
* ❖ Carbohydrates: 5g
* ❖ Sugars: 2g
* ❖ Protein: 4g
* ❖ Dietary Fiber: 1g

Ingredients

* ❖ 2 large tomatoes cut into thick slices (about 1 inch)
* ❖ 1/3 cup shredded cheese (try parmesan, Swiss, or cheddar)
* ❖ 1 teaspoon dried oregano
* ❖ 1/4 teaspoon each salt and pepper
* ❖ 1/4 teaspoon garlic powder (1 clove garlic, minced)

Directions

- ❖ Preheat oven to 400 degrees. Place tomato slices in a single layer in a shallow baking dish.
- ❖ In a small bowl, combine cheese, oregano, salt, pepper, and garlic powder. Sprinkle mixture over tomatoes.
- ❖ Bake 5 to 10 minutes, or until cheese turns golden brown and starts to bubble. Serve warm.

---

32.   Pinto Bean Dip

Prep Time: 5 minutes

Makes: 3 1/4 cups

Nutritional Facts

- ❖ Calories: 35
- ❖ Calories From Fat 10
- ❖ Total Fat: 1g
- ❖ Sodium: 70mg
- ❖ Carbohydrates: 5g
- ❖ Sugars: 1g
- ❖ Protein: 1g
- ❖ Dietary Fiber: 0g

Ingredients

- ❖ 1 can (15 ounces) pinto beans, rinsed and drained
- ❖ 1 can (4 ounces) mild jalapeño peppers
- ❖ 1 tablespoon vegetable oil
- ❖ 1 tablespoon barbecue sauce or ketchup
- ❖ 1 tablespoon water
- ❖ ½ teaspoon onion powder
- ❖ ⅛ teaspoon each salt and pepper

Instructions

- ❖ For a smooth dip, place ingredients in a blender and blend until smooth.
- ❖ For a chunky dip, mash beans well with a fork or potato masher, stir in remaining ingredients.
- ❖ Add additional water as needed for desired consistency.
- ❖ Refrigerate leftovers within 2 hours.

Notes

- ❖ Serve with fresh vegetables or Food Hero Baked Tortilla Chips.
- ❖ Cook your own dry beans. One can (15 ounces) is about 1 1/2 to 1 3/4 cups drained beans.

Dessert Recipes

---

33.   Almond Rice Pudding

Prep Time: 5 minutes

Cooking Time: 30 minutes

Makes: 3 cups

Nutritional Facts

* ❖ Calories: 180
* ❖ Calories From Fat: 5
* ❖ Total Fat: 1.5g
* ❖ Sodium: 75mg

- ❖ Carbohydrates: 37g
- ❖ Sugars: 12g
- ❖ Protein: 3g
- ❖ Dietary Fiber: 1g
- ❖ Cholesterol: 0mg

Ingredients

- ❖ 3 cups almond milk
- ❖ 1 cup white or brown rice, uncooked
- ❖ 1/4 cup sugar
- ❖ 1 teaspoon vanilla
- ❖ 1/4 teaspoon almond extract
- ❖ cinnamon to taste
- ❖ 1/4 cup toasted almonds (optional)

Directions

- ❖ Combine almond milk and rice in a 2-3 quart saucepan, and bring to a boil.
- ❖ Reduce heat and simmer for 1/2 hour with the lid on until the rice is soft.
- ❖ Add sugar, vanilla, almond extract, and cinnamon. Stir and serve warm.
- ❖ Refrigerate leftovers within 2 hours.

Notes

- ❖ Add your favorite berries to the top for some color and a yummy taste!
- ❖ Add an extra cup of almond milk for a creamier texture.
- ❖ No almond milk? Use non-fat or 1% milk and 1½ teaspoons almond extract.

---

34.   Winter Fruit Crisp

Prep Time: 5 minutes

Cooking Time: 30 minutes

Makes: 8 Bars (4 inches x 2 inches)

Nutritional Facts

- ❖ Calories: 260
- ❖ Calories From Fat: 70
- ❖ Total Fat: 8g
- ❖ Sodium: 95mg
- ❖ Carbohydrates: 48g
- ❖ Sugars: 33g
- ❖ Protein: 2g
- ❖ Dietary Fiber: 3g
- ❖ Cholesterol: 0mg

Ingredients

- ❖ 4 cups diced apples or pears
- ❖ 2/3 cup packed brown sugar
- ❖ ½ cup all-purpose flour
- ❖ ½ cup old fashioned rolled oats
- ❖ 1/3 cup margarine
- ❖ 1 teaspoon cinnamon

Instructions

- ❖ Heat oven to 375 degrees. Lightly spray or oil a square pan (8 x 8 x 2 inches).
- ❖ Arrange fruit in pan. Mix remaining ingredients and sprinkle over fruit.
- ❖ Bake until topping is golden brown and fruit is tender, about 30 minutes.
- ❖ Refrigerate leftovers within 2 hours.

Notes

- ❖ Use any fresh, frozen or drained canned fruit that you have on hand.
- ❖ Add 1/2 cup of dried fruit (raisins, cranberries, cut apricots).
- ❖ Try vanilla yogurt as a topping and sprinkle with cinnamon.

35.   Bread Pudding in The Microwave

Prep Time: 5 minutes

Cooking Time: 10 minutes

Makes: 3 Cups

Nutritional Facts

❖ Calories: 210

❖ Calories From Fat: 45

❖ Total Fat: 5g

❖ Sodium: 240mg

- ❖ Carbohydrates: 35g
- ❖ Sugars: 29g
- ❖ Protein: 7g
- ❖ Dietary Fiber: 2g
- ❖ Cholesterol: 95mg

Ingredients

- ❖ 1 tablespoon butter or margarine
- ❖ 3 slices whole grain bread
- ❖ ½ cup packed brown sugar
- ❖ ½ cup raisins
- ❖ 3 eggs, slightly beaten
- ❖ 1 ¼ cups nonfat or 1% milk
- ❖ 1 teaspoon cinnamon
- ❖ ¼ teaspoon salt
- ❖ 1 teaspoon vanilla

Instructions

- ❖ Butter bread and cut into small cubes.
- ❖ Combine buttered and cubed bread, brown sugar and raisins in a one-quart microwave safe dish.
- ❖ In a microwave safe bowl or measuring cup, blend together the eggs, milk, cinnamon, salt, and vanilla.
- ❖ Heat on high for 2-3 minutes until hot, but not boiling.

- ❖ Pour over bread mixture and lightly blend together.
- ❖ Microwave uncovered at 50% power for 5-8 minutes, or until edges are firm and the center is almost set.
- ❖ Let rest for 10 minutes before serving.
- ❖ Refrigerate leftovers within 2 hours.

Notes

- ❖ Serve with low-fat vanilla or lemon yogurt.

---

36.   Baked Apple And Cranberries

Prep Time: 5 minutes

Cooking Time: 5 minutes

Makes: 1 Apple

Nutritional Facts

* Calories: 150
* Calories From Fat: 20
* Total Fat: 2g
* Sodium: 240mg
* Carbohydrates: 35g
* Sugars: 28g
* Protein: 0g
* Dietary Fiber: 5g
* Cholesterol: 0mg

Ingredients

* 1 baking apple (try Golden Delicious, Granny Smith, Jonathan, or Braeburn)
* dash of cinnamon to taste
* 1 Tablespoon dried cranberries
* 1 teaspoon brown sugar
* 1/2 teaspoon margarine

Directions

* Wash the apple and remove the core (seed area), leaving the bottom to hold in the filling.

- ❖ Peel a small band of skin from around the top of the apple.
- ❖ Place the apple in a microwave-safe container.
- ❖ Sprinkle cinnamon around the top of the apple and into the hole.
- ❖ Fill the center of the apple with cranberries, pressing down if needed.
- ❖ Top the cranberries with brown sugar and margarine.
- ❖ Cover loosely with wax paper.
- ❖ Microwave on high for about 2 1/2 minutes or until apple is soft when poked through the center hole with a fork. Cool slightly.
- ❖ Refrigerate leftovers within 2 hours.

Notes

- ❖ Try using a corer or a paring knife and a small melon baller or the tip of a vegetable peeler to remove the core.
- ❖ Try fresh cranberries, raisins, or other dry fruit in the center.
- ❖ For additional servings, increase the cooking time to about 1 minute for each apple.
- ❖ Serve for breakfast or dessert!

Prep Time: 15 minutes

Cooking Time: 45 minutes

Makes: 5 cups

Nutritional Facts

- ❖ Calories: 240
- ❖ Calories From Fat: 50
- ❖ Total Fat: 6g
- ❖ Sodium: 65mg
- ❖ Carbohydrates: 46g

- ❖ Sugars: 32g

- ❖ Protein: 2g

- ❖ Dietary Fiber: 3g

- ❖ Cholesterol: 0mg

Ingredients

Topping

- ❖ ½ cup packed brown sugar

- ❖ ½ cup flour

- ❖ ½ cup old fashioned rolled oats

- ❖ ¼ cup melted margarine

Fruit Filling

- ❖ 3 cups chopped rhubarb

- ❖ 3 cups blueberries

- ❖ 2 tablespoons cornstarch

- ❖ ½ cup sugar

- ❖ 1 cup cranberry juice

- ❖ 1 teaspoon vanilla

Instructions

- ❖ Mix the brown sugar, flour and oats in a bowl. Stir in the margarine. Set aside.

- ❖ Spread the rhubarb and blueberries in an 8-inch baking dish.
- ❖ In a 2-3 quart saucepan, mix cornstarch and sugar and stir in the juice. Cook over medium heat until thickened, stirring constantly.
- ❖ Add the vanilla and pour mixture over the rhubarb and blueberries.
- ❖ Crumble the oat mixture on top of the fruit.
- ❖ Bake at 350 degrees for 45 minutes.
- ❖ Serve warm or cold. Refrigerate leftovers within 2 hours.

Notes

- ❖ Try strawberries instead of blueberries.
- ❖ Use apple or grape juice instead of cranberry juice.

---

38.   Pumpkin Fruit Dip

Prep Time: 5 minutes

Makes: 3 cups

Nutritional Facts

- ❖ Calories: 40
- ❖ Calories From Fat: 5
- ❖ Total Fat: 0.5g

- ❖ Sodium: 25mg
- ❖ Carbohydrates: 8g
- ❖ Sugars: 7g
- ❖ Protein: 1g
- ❖ Dietary Fiber: 1g
- ❖ Cholesterol: 5mg

Ingredients

- ❖ 1 can (15 ounce) pumpkin (about 1 ¾ cups cooked pumpkin)
- ❖ 1 cup low-fat ricotta cheese or plain yogurt or low-fat cream cheese
- ❖ ¾ cup sugar
- ❖ 1 ½ teaspoons cinnamon
- ❖ ½ teaspoon nutmeg

Instructions

- ❖ In a large bowl, combine pumpkin, ricotta cheese or yogurt or cream cheese, cinnamon and nutmeg. Add sugar a little at a time to reach desired sweetness. Stir until smooth.
- ❖ Refrigerate leftovers within 2 hours.
- ❖ Notes
- ❖ Serve with apple slices, bananas or grapes.

- ❖ Try using a mixture of ricotta, yogurt, or cream cheese.
- ❖ For a smoother texture, use a hand mixer or food processor to mix ingredients.

---

39.   Cherry Oat Crumble

Prep Time: 15 minutes

Cooking Time: 45 minutes

Makes: 3 cups

Nutritional Facts

- ❖ Calories: 210
- ❖ Calories From Fat: 5
- ❖ Total Fat: 5g
- ❖ Sodium: 85mg
- ❖ Carbohydrates: 42g
- ❖ Sugars: 29g
- ❖ Protein: 3g
- ❖ Dietary Fiber: 3g
- ❖ Cholesterol: 0mg

Ingredients

- ❖ 6 Tablespoons sugar
- ❖ 1 1/2 Tablespoons cornstarch
- ❖ 4 cups tart cherries, pitted, fresh or frozen
- ❖ 3/4 teaspoon vanilla
- ❖ 6 Tablespoons whole wheat flour
- ❖ 6 Tablespoons old fashioned rolled oats
- ❖ 3 Tablespoons brown sugar
- ❖ 1/8 teaspoon salt
- ❖ 2 Tablespoons butter or margarine, melted

Directions

- ❖ Preheat the oven to 350° F.
- ❖ Mix the sugar and cornstarch in a large bowl.

- ❖ Add the cherries and stir to mix. Add the vanilla and mix again.

- ❖ Pour the fruit into an 8 x 8 baking pan or 2-quart casserole.

- ❖ In a separate bowl mix together the flour, oats, brown sugar, and salt. Add the melted butter and mix until the texture is coarse with some clumps. Distribute the oat topping over the fruit.

- ❖ Bake in the preheated oven for about 30-45 minutes, or until the juices are bubbling and the oat topping is golden brown.

- ❖ Refrigerate leftovers within 2 hours

40.   Pumpkin Pudding

Prep Time: 10 minutes

Makes: 4 cups

Nutritional Facts

- ❖ Calories: 100
- ❖ Calories From Fat: 10
- ❖ Total Fat: 1g
- ❖ Sodium: 270mg
- ❖ Carbohydrates: 21g
- ❖ Sugars: 18g
- ❖ Protein: 3g
- ❖ Dietary Fiber: 3g

* Cholesterol: 5mg

Ingredients

* 1 can (15 ounces) pumpkin or 2 cups cooked mashed squash (such as Hubbard)
* ⅛ teaspoon salt
* 2 teaspoons pumpkin pie spice (or 1 teaspoon cinnamon, 1/2 teaspoon ginger, 1/4 teaspoon nutmeg and 1/4 teaspoon cloves)
* 1 ½ cups nonfat or 1% milk
* 1 package (makes 4 servings) instant vanilla pudding mix

Instructions

* In a large bowl, mix pumpkin, salt and pumpkin pie spice together.
* Slowly stir in milk and mix well.
* Add instant pudding mix and stir for 2 minutes until it thickens.
* Refrigerate until serving time.
* Refrigerate leftovers within 2 hours.

Drinks Recipes

41. Apple Cinnamon Flavored Water

Prep Time: 5 minutes

Chill Time: 3 hours to overnight

Makes: 4 cups

Nutritional Facts

❖ Calories: 80kcal

❖ Carbohydrates: 3g

❖ Protein: 1g

❖ Fat: 1g

❖ Saturated Fat: 1g

- ❖ Sodium: 12mg
- ❖ Potassium: 37mg
- ❖ Fiber: 1g
- ❖ Sugar: 1g
- ❖ Vitamin C: 14mg
- ❖ Calcium: 14mg
- ❖ Iron: 1mg

Ingredients

- ❖ 1/2 apple
- ❖ 1/2 cinnamon stick
- ❖ 4 cups of water

Directions

- ❖ Wash the apple thoroughly under cool running water.
- ❖ Slice the apple into thin slices or circles, leaving the skin and core or removing either or both.
- ❖ Add the apple slices and cinnamon stick to the water and refrigerate several hours or overnight to allow the most flavoring, then keep it cold to keep it safe.
- ❖ Drink within 2 days for best quality.

Notes

❖ Keep it Safe! Do not mix batches of flavored water. Use it up, clean the container, then make a new batch.

42.   Citrus Cucumber Water

Prep Time: 10 minutes

Chill Time: 2 hours

Makes: 8 cups

Nutritional Facts

❖ Calories: 109kcal
❖ Carbohydrates: 30g
❖ Protein: 1g
❖ Sodium: 12mg
❖ Fiber: 1g
❖ Sugar: 26g

Ingredients

❖ 1 large lemon
❖ 1 large lime
❖ 1 large orange
❖ 1 large cucumber
❖ 8 cups cold water

Directions

- ❖ Scrub all fruits and cucumber thoroughly under running water.
- ❖ Cut the citrus fruit into thin slices, with or without peeling, and put in a pitcher.
- ❖ Peel the cucumber and cut into thin slices, with or without peeling. Add cucumber slices to fruit slices in the pitcher.
- ❖ Add water, stir well and refrigerate for 2 hours before serving, then keep it cold to keep it safe.
- ❖ Drink within 2 days for best quality.

Notes

- ❖ Keep it Safe! Do not mix batches of flavored water. Use it up, clean the container, then make a fresh batch.

43. Citrus Flavored Water

Prep Time: 5 minutes

Chill Time: 3 hours to overnight

Makes: 4 cups

Nutritional Facts

- ❖ Calories 130
- ❖ Calories from Fat 9
- ❖ Fat 1g
- ❖ Saturated Fat 1g
- ❖ Sodium 11mg
- ❖ Potassium 29mg

- ❖ Carbohydrates 1g
- ❖ Fiber 1g
- ❖ Sugar 1g
- ❖ Protein 1g
- ❖ Vitamin A 127IU
- ❖ Vitamin C 1mg
- ❖ Calcium 13mg
- ❖ Iron 1mg

Ingredients

- ❖ 1/2 small or 1/4 large citrus fruit (lemon, lime, orange, or grapefruit)
- ❖ 4 cups of water

Directions

- ❖ Scrub the fruit thoroughly under cool running water.
- ❖ Slice the fruit thinly into whole circles or quarter wedges, with or without the skin.
- ❖ Add fruit slices to water and refrigerate several hours to overnight to allow the most flavoring, then keep it cold to keep it safe.
- ❖ Drink within 2 days for best quality.

Notes

❖ Keep it Safe! Do not mix batches of flavored water. Use it up, clean the container, then make a fresh batch.

---

44. Cucumber Flavored Water

Prep Time: 5 minutes

Chill Time: 3 hours to overnight

Makes: 4 cups

Nutritional Facts

❖ Calories: 133

- ❖ Total fat: 1g
- ❖ Unsaturated fat: 0g
- ❖ Sodium: 33mg
- ❖ Carbohydrates: 33g
- ❖ Fiber: 5g
- ❖ Sugar: 17g
- ❖ Protein: 5g

Ingredients

- ❖ 1/2 cucumber
- ❖ 1-quart water

Directions

- ❖ Scrub the cucumber thoroughly under cool running water.
- ❖ Cut the cucumber into thin slices, with or without skin.
- ❖ add cucumber slices to water and refrigerate several hours to overnight to allow the most flavoring, then keep it cold to keep it safe.
- ❖ Drink within 2 days for best quality.

Notes

Keep it Safe! Do not mix batches of flavored water. Use it up, clean the container, then make a fresh batch.

45. Glass of Sunshine Flavored Water

Prep Time: 5 minutes

Chill Time: 2 hours

Makes: 8 cups

Nutritional Facts

❖ Calories: 67kcal

❖ Carbohydrates: 1g

❖ Fat: 1g

❖ Sodium: 1mg

❖ Sugar:13g

Ingredients

❖ 1 orange

❖ 2 quarts water

Directions

❖ Scrub the orange thoroughly under cool running water.

❖ Slice the orange into thin slices, with or without the peel.

❖ Combine the orange slices and water in a pitcher and refrigerate for 2 hours before serving.

❖ Drink within 2 days for best quality.

Notes

❖ Keep It Safe! Do not mix batches of flavored water. Use it up, clean the container, then make a fresh batch.

---

46.   Herb Flavored Water

Prep Time: 5 minutes

Chill Time: 3 hours to overnight

Makes: 4 cups

Nutritional Facts

- ❖ Protein: 1g
- ❖ Carbohydrates: 15.1g
- ❖ Dietary Fiber: 0.2g
- ❖ Sugars: 1g
- ❖ Vitamin A Iu: 10.2IU
- ❖ Vitamin B: 2mg
- ❖ Vitamin C: 6.1mg
- ❖ Calcium: 11.2mg
- ❖ Iron: 3mg
- ❖ Magnesium: 4mg
- ❖ Potassium: 26mg

Ingredients

- ❖ 10 small leaves or a small sprig of herb (mint, basil, or rosemary)
- ❖ 4 cups of water

Directions

- ❖ Wash the herbs thoroughly under cool running water.
- ❖ Tear or crush the herb leaves.
- ❖ Add herb to water and refrigerate several hours or overnight to allow the most flavoring, then keep it cold to keep it safe.
- ❖ Drink within 2 days for best quality.

Notes

❖ Keep it Safe! Do not mix batches of flavored water. Use it up, clean the container, then make a fresh batch.

---

47.   Peachy Keen Flavored Water

Prep Time: 10 minutes (plus time to freeze ice cubes)

Makes: 6 fluid ounces + ice cubes

Nutritional Facts

❖ Calories: 174.7

❖ Protein: 1.8g

❖ Carbohydrates: 42.8g

❖ Dietary Fiber: 1.4g

❖ Sugars: 38.1g

❖ Vitamin A Iu: 806.6IU

❖ Vitamin B6: 0.1mg

❖ Vitamin C: 101.9mg

❖ Calcium: 28.9mg

❖ Iron: 0.7mg

❖ Magnesium: 27.2mg

❖ Potassium: 439.4mg

Ingredients

- ❖ 3/4 cup pureed peach, fresh or frozen and thawed
- ❖ 4 cups cold water
- ❖ 1 tray of regular or sage leaf ice cubes

Directions

- ❖ Combine peach puree and water in a pitcher.
- ❖ Add ice cubes.
- ❖ Stir well and serve immediately for best quality.
- ❖ Keep it cold to keep it save and refrigerate any leftovers within 2 hours.

To Make Sage Leaf Ice Cubes:

- ❖ Place a thoroughly washed sage leaf into each ice cube tray hole.
- ❖ Fill the holes up halfway with tap water and freeze solid.
- ❖ After the ice is set, fill the top half of the holes with water. This allows the sage leaves to be frozen in the middle of the ice cube instead of at the top.

Notes

Keep it Safe! Do not mix batches of flavored water. Use it up, clean the container, then make a fresh batch.

48.   Strawberry Kiwi Flavored Water

Prep Time: 10 minutes

Chill Time: 3 to 12 hours

Makes: 4 cups

Nutritional Facts

❖ Calories: 268.5
❖ Protein: 6.6g
❖ Carbohydrates: 61g
❖ Sugars: 49.3g
❖ Fat: 1.9g
❖ Vitamin A Iu: 242.1IU

- ❖ Vitamin B6: 0.3mg
- ❖ Vitamin C: 113.6mg
- ❖ Calcium: 192.2mg
- ❖ Iron: 0.8mg
- ❖ Magnesium: 53.5mg
- ❖ Potassium: 773mg
- ❖ Sodium: 64.5mg

Ingredients

- ❖ 4 strawberries
- ❖ 1/2 kiwi
- ❖ 4 cups of water

Directions

- ❖ Wash and trim away the core and any bruised areas of the strawberries. Wash and peel the kiwi.
- ❖ Slice both fruits into thin slices.
- ❖ Add fruit to water and refrigerate for several hours to overnight to allow the most flavoring, then keep it cold to keep it safe.
- ❖ Drink within 2 days for best quality.

Notes

Keep It Safe! Do not mix batches of flavored water. Use it up, clean the container, then make a fresh batch.

CPSIA information can be obtained
at www.ICGtesting.com
Printed in the USA
BVHW060035280221
601200BV00001B/65